# *Arts & Crafts*

# KNITTING
# AND CROCHET

## Susie O'Reilly

*With photographs by Zul Mukhida*

Thomson Learning

New York

**Books in this series**

BATIK AND TIE-DYE
BLOCK PRINTING
KNITTING AND CROCHET
MODELING
NEEDLECRAFT
PAPERMAKING
STENCILS AND SCREENS
WEAVING

Title page *A detail of work by Kaffe Fassett, who uses soft colors and intricate patterns to create beautiful effects in knitting. In the twentieth century, knitting has often been seen as women's work, but Kaffe Fassett has become famous as a talented male knitwear designer.*

First published in the
United States in 1994 by
Thomson Learning
115 Fifth Avenue
New York, NY 10003

Published simultaneously in
Great Britain by
Wayland (Publishers) Ltd.

Library of Congress Cataloging-in-Publication Data
O'Reilly, Susie, 1949-
    Knitting and crochet/Susie O'Reilly; with photographs
by Zul Mukhida.
        p.    cm.—(Arts & crafts)
    Includes bibliographical references and index.
    ISBN 1-56847-221-8
    1. Knitting—Juvenile literature. 2. Crocheting—Juvenile
literature. [1. Knitting. 2 Crocheting.] I. Mukhida, Zul, ill.
II. Title. III. Series: O'Reilly, Susie, 1949– Arts & crafts.
TT820.066        1994
746.43—dc20                                    94-12199

Printed in Italy

# CONTENTS

Words printed in **bold** appear in the glossary.

# GETTING STARTED

There are three main ways of making fabric (cloth) from **fibers**: **felting**, **weaving,** and knitting. Crochet is a technique similar to knitting. Several things make knitting and crochet different from other ways of making cloth. First, just one long piece of yarn is used and made into a series of interconnecting loops, using one or more **needles**. Second, woven and felted cloth are made and then cut to the required shape, but knitted and crocheted cloth can be shaped as it is made.

Crochet can be done only by hand. Knitting, however, can be done by hand or machine. It can be a relaxing hobby, a small business employing a few people to produce hand-knitted clothes, or a major part of the **textiles** industry. Remember that knitting is not just about making woolly sweaters and winter scarves. All kinds of fibers can be knitted. T-shirts, for example, are usually made from knitted cotton, which produces a very soft, comfortable cloth.

▲ *A traditional crocheted shawl of fine, soft wool from the Scottish island of Shetland.*

◀ *This piece, by Sue Black, combines knitting and embroidery to create an abstract effect.*

From time to time, **fashion designers** take up the hand-knitted look. During the early 1980s hand-knitted sweaters in bright colors and jazzy patterns were popular. In the early 1990s, crocheted vests became fashionable.

# SETTING UP YOUR WORK AREA

You will need to collect these tools and materials to get started.

**Needles**
Metal or plastic crochet
  hooks, in various sizes
Some pairs of knitting
  needles, large and small
  (No. 10 needles are large,
  No. 6 ones are medium)
Tapestry needles, with
  large eyes and blunt
  points, for sewing up
  finished work

**Fibers and yarns**
An assortment of wool and
  other yarns in a range of
  colors and thicknesses
  (including some string,
  leather, plastic, raffia,
  ribbon, and silk)

*Today,* ▶
*chunky hand-
knitted sweaters
are fashionable
as well as being
warm and
comfortable.*

**Decoration**
A variety of beads, buttons,
  and found objects (such
  as small shells, pebbles,
  and bottle tops) to sew
  onto your work

▼ *Knitting yarns come in
different thicknesses.*

**General equipment**
Scissors
Dressmaker's pins
A camera, notebook, and
  colored markers or crayons
Graph paper

Note: Knitting yarns are sold in various thicknesses – you will see yarns marked "2-ply" (which is very thin), "4-ply," and "sport yarn," for example. If you want to use more than one yarn in a piece of work (to change color, for instance), you must make sure that all the yarns are the same thickness. If you use more than one skein of the same color yarn, it is important that the dye lot numbers match.

# KNITTING AND CROCHET IN OTHER TIMES

Compared with weaving and felting, which have been used to make cloth for many thousands of years, hand knitting is a fairly recent craft. Little is known about how or when it first developed. Most people agree that knitting probably started in Egypt, perhaps as recently as A.D. 400. Some examples of early Egyptian knitting still exist today and are on display in museums.

During the **Middle Ages**, knitting spread from Egypt to Europe. Sailors from Europe picked up the skill on their travels to foreign lands and passed on their knowledge when they returned home. This is why there is a strong **tradition** of knitting in many fishing villages in Europe.

▲ *This pair of socks is an example of very early knitting from Egypt.*

The earliest examples of European knitting come from **medieval** Spain – two knitted cushions found in the tombs of a monastery. In the early fourteenth century, in northern Italy and Germany, painters sometimes showed Mary, the mother of Jesus Christ, at work knitting a sweater, in their pictures.

◄ *This German altarpiece, painted in about 1390, shows the Virgin Mary knitting a sweater.*

▲ *A man's knitted hat from sixteenth-century England.*

By the sixteenth century, knitting had become an important craft all over Europe. In Great Britain, for example, the knitting industry was organized into **guilds** of master craftsmen. Only men who had served a long **apprenticeship** and who could prove their skills by passing a difficult exam were allowed to work as **professional** knitters.

However, in the fishing villages of northern Europe – in Scotland and Scandinavia – women continued to knit sweaters at home. In Scotland, women knitted sweaters known as ganseys for their husbands and sons. Ganseys were knitted in complicated patterns. Each pattern belonged to a particular family or village.

Toward the end of World War I (1914-18), sailors from the United States Navy were sent to Fair Isle, a small island off the north coast of Scotland. The sailors sent traditional Fair Isle sweaters to friends in England and the United States, where they became very fashionable. In the 1920s the Prince of Wales (later Edward VIII of Great Britain) started to wear Fair Isle sweaters. The prince was a leader of fashion, and the sweaters became enormously popular.

*This* ▶ *photograph, from the 1950s, shows a Scottish woman knitting and carrying home a basket of peat.*

*Traditional Fair Isle-patterned sweaters are still produced* ◀ *today.*

Crochet was popular in the nineteenth century and became really fashionable during World War I. It was considered a suitable occupation for young women, who crocheted edgings for household linen such as pillowcases and tablecloths. Mothers made crocheted shawls and clothes for their babies. Crocheted collars were a fashionable way of trimming a plain dress. Women's magazines encouraged this fashion by printing crochet **patterns**.

# THE DEVELOPMENT OF TOOLS

The earliest knitting needles had a hook at one end, like a modern crochet hook, for catching the yarn. These were later replaced by straight needles, like our modern ones. Hooked needles are still used today in some Egyptian villages. The first straight needles were made from a variety of materials, such as metal, wood, and **ivory**. They were often made by the knitters themselves, who took great care of them. Cork or wooden stoppers were used to protect the points and they were wrapped in leather folders or kept in carved wooden cases.

The native peoples of North America wove fabrics on sticks stuck into the ground. A thread was wound in and out of the sticks to make a tube of cloth. This type of weaving is similar to spool knitting. Four nails are hammered into a thread spool, and nails are used to "knit" the yarn. Children still spool knit to make long knitted cords, bracelets, and neckties.

◀ *Today, knitting needles and crochet hooks are usually made from plastic, aluminum, or wood.*

Knitters were always looking for ways of working more quickly. Many professional knitters used a knitting **sheath** to hold the right-hand needle, leaving that hand free to push the stitches from one needle to the other. With the help of a sheath, a really fast knitter could make 100 stitches or more a minute.

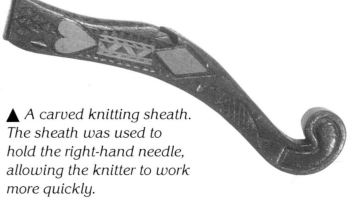

▲ *A carved knitting sheath. The sheath was used to hold the right-hand needle, allowing the knitter to work more quickly.*

*◄ A knitting doll – medieval knitting machines worked in the same way.*

*Greek ► women producing traditional crochet.*

The medieval European knitting frame also used this idea. Pegs were set around a central hole. The yarn was wound around the pegs to form a variety of stitches and, as it grew, the tube of knitting was fed down through the hole. A frame like this was particularly useful for knitting socks and stockings.

Compared to knitting, the tools used for crochet have changed little over the centuries. The first crochet hooks were made by hand from wood, bone, or ivory. Today, they are most likely to be made of plastic or aluminum.

*▼ Modern knitting machines speed up the knitting process.*

The first knitting machine was invented in 1589 in Cambridge, England, by a man named William Lee. Lee used to watch his wife knitting. He realized that, by using two needles, only one stitch could be made at a time. But if a whole row of needles were used, then a whole row of knitting could be done at once. The highly complicated knitting machines used by the textiles industry today are based on this idea. These machines are controlled by computer and can produce knitted cloth at incredible speed.

# CASTING ON AND MAKING STITCHES

## CASTING ON

**1** Take a piece of yarn and make a **slipknot** in the end of it.

**2** Slide the loop onto the needle in your left hand.

**3** Put the needle in your right hand into the front of the loop.

**4** Bring the yarn around from the back to the front of the right needle, pulling it between the two needles.

**5** Slide the right needle back and down, turning it toward you so that the yarn is pulled through to make a second loop.

**6** Slip the loop onto the left needle. You have made your first stitch. There are now two stitches on the left needle.

**7** Now make a third stitch. Put the right needle in between the first and the second stitch. Repeat steps 4–6. You now have three stitches.

**8** Continue making stitches in the way you made the third stitch, until you have as many on the left needle as you need.

# KNITTING THE FIRST ROW

**1** With the yarn at the back of your work, put the right needle into the front, or bottom, of the first stitch.

*Keep knitting extra rows and watch your work grow!* ▶

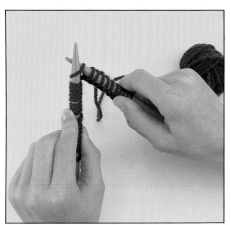

**2** Bring the yarn around between the two needles.

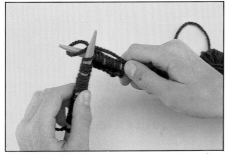

**3** Slide the right needle back and down, twisting it to catch the yarn as a loop.

**4** Keeping this loop on the right needle, slip the first stitch off the left needle. You have made a stitch.

**5** Repeat steps 1–4 until all the stitches have been transferred from the left needle to the right needle.

Note: Knitting is usually worked from right to left. If you are left-handed, you may want to work this way. Or you may want to hold the needle with the stitches in your right hand and knit onto the needle in your left hand. If so, reverse these instructions, reading "left" for "right" and "right" for "left." Hold the pictures up to a mirror and use the reflection.

# KNITTING THE SECOND ROW

**1** Place the right needle, with the stitches, into your left hand. Pick up the empty needle in your right hand.

**2** Repeating steps 1–5 for knitting the first row, make a second row.

**3** To make further rows, keep swapping the needles at the end of each row and repeating steps 1–5.

# MAKING DIFFERENT STITCHES AND ADDING COLOR

So far, each time you have made a stitch, you have put your needle into the front of the loop. This is called plain knitting. In knitting instructions, plain stitches are always called "knit" stitches. However, there are many different ways of making stitches.

## PURL STITCH

**1** Keep the yarn at the front of the work. Put your right needle into the top of the stitch on the left needle, *from right to left.*

**2** Bring the yarn between the needles and around the right needle. Twist through to make a stitch on the right needle. Slip the first stitch off the left needle.

## RIBBING

**1** Row 1: Knit one plain stitch, take the yarn between the needles to the front of the work, then purl one stitch. Take the yarn to the back and repeat.

**2** Row 2: Purl each stitch that was knit plain in row 1, and knit each stitch that was purl. Take the yarn to the front or back of the work between each stitch.

Repeat these two rows.

◀ *Ribbing produces a stretchy effect, which is useful on the cuffs or the bottom of a sweater.*

## GARTER STITCH

Knit every row in plain stitch. Your knitting will look the same on both sides (you get the same result if you purl every row).

## STOCKING STITCH

Knit one row plain and one row purl, alternately. Your knitting will have a smooth look on one side and a more textured look on the other side.

▼ *Stocking stitch (top) and garter stitch (bottom).*

# MAKING COLORED STRIPES

**1** Knit one or more rows in your first color.

**2** Change the yarn to knit one or more rows in a second color. To change the yarn at the beginning of a row, knit the first five stitches using the first color *and* the second color. Then continue with the second color.

**3** Use as many different colors as you want, and knit as many or as few rows in each color as you like, to make thick or thin stripes.

**4** When you have finished the piece of knitting, clean up all the loose ends. Using a tapestry needle, sew the tail of each color into the back of your work. Remember to leave a long enough tail of yarn to thread the sewing needle!

# CHANGING COLOR IN THE ROW

You can build up patterns and pictures in a piece of knitting by changing the color of yarn anywhere along the row.

**1** First, plan the pattern on graph paper. Color the squares to represent the different colored yarns you will use.

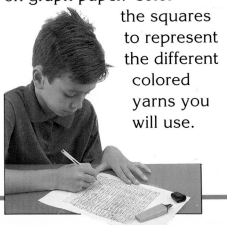

**2** Knit the pattern, changing color as necessary.

Carry the various colored yarns along the back of the work, twisting the yarns around each other every now and then. The carried yarns are called floats.

Note: If you use more than one yarn, make sure all the yarns are of the same thickness – otherwise your work will not come out the correct shape.

# SHAPING AND FINISHING WORK

Knitted fabric cannot easily be cut into shape, because it will **unravel**. However, by **increasing** and **decreasing** the number of stitches in each row, you can shape the work as you go along.

Then, when you have finished knitting and want to complete your work, you need to make a row that will not unravel. This is called casting off.

## INCREASING

**1** Put the right needle into the front of the stitch. Bring the yarn around between the needles to make a loop. Keep the loop on the right needle but do not allow the old stitch to slip off the left needle.

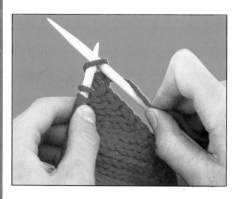

**2** Put the right needle into the back of the same stitch. Bring the yarn around between the needles, make a loop, and slip the first

stitch off the left needle. You have made two stitches from the one stitch.

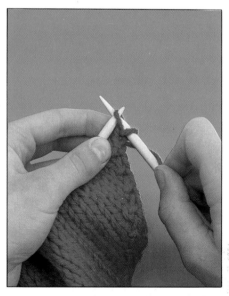

**3** You can increase in this way by making extra stitches at the beginning or end of a row, or at intervals along the row.

## DECREASING

**1** Knit two stitches together. Place the point of the right needle in the front of two stitches at the same time.

**2** Make a normal stitch. You will only have one stitch where you had two. Decrease in this way at the beginning or end of the row, or at intervals along the row.

# CASTING OFF

1 Knit the first two stitches of the row as usual, so that there are two stitches on the right needle.

2 Use the point of the left needle to lift the first stitch over the second. Allow the loop to fall off the needle.

3 Knit another stitch and then repeat step 2.

4 Continue until you have the final stitch on the right needle. Cut the yarn, leaving an end of about 6 inches. Bring the end through the loop of the final stitch and pull gently. This makes the stitch secure.

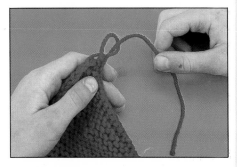

*Shape* ▶ *your work by increasing or decreasing stitches.*

Note: Take special care when washing any work made of wool. Wool **shrinks** if it is washed in hot water, so use cool water. Dry woolen objects by squeezing out as much water as possible, gently pulling it into shape and drying flat. Do not hang up to dry.

# SEWING UP

1 Cover each piece of knitting with a damp cloth and press flat with a warm iron. **Ask an adult to help you with the iron**.

2 Use a tapestry needle to sew any loose ends into the back of the work.

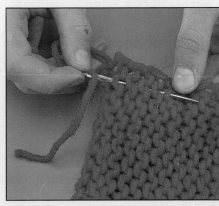

3 Thread a tapestry needle with a piece of the yarn you have been knitting with. Place the pieces to be sewn with **right sides** together. Sew the pieces together along the **seams** by catching a thread from each side alternately.

# BASIC CROCHET

## CASTING ON

Make a small slipknot by twisting the yarn around the crochet hook and pulling a loop through with the hook. Place the loop on the hook.

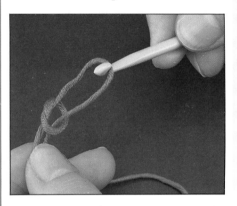

## CHAIN STITCH

1 Hold the hook with the slipknot on it in your right hand. Grab the yarn in your left hand and make a fist.

2 Point your left-hand forefinger at your chest and bring it up under the yarn between your fist and the hook. Keep it taught.

3 Hold the tail between your middle finger and thumb of your left hand.

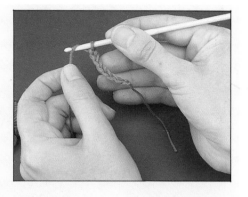

4 Take the yarn over the hook from the back and draw the hook through the loop to make a chain stitch.

5 Repeat steps 3–4 to make a length of stitches.

## SINGLE CROCHET

1 Make a foundation chain. Count back to the second to last chain stitch.

3 Bring the yarn over the hook and draw a loop through. There are now two loops on the hook.

4 Bring the yarn over the hook again and draw a loop through both loops on the hook.

5 The first single crochet stitch is now complete. Insert the hook through the next stitch back. Repeat steps 3–4 to make the next stitch. Continue until you reach the end of the row.

6 Now work one chain stitch. This is called the turning chain. To start the second row, turn the work in order to crochet back in the other direction.

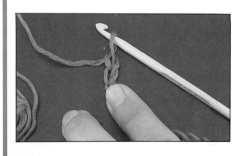

2 Insert the hook through this stitch, from front to back.

# DOUBLE CROCHET

**1** Before beginning a row of double crochet, work a turning chain of three chain stitches.

**2** Bring the yarn over the hook. There are now two loops on the hook. Insert the hook into the second stitch of the previous row.

**3** Bring the yarn over the hook again and draw it through this stitch. There are now three loops on the hook.

**4** Bring the yarn over the hook and draw it through the first two loops.

**5** Again bring the yarn over the hook and draw it through the remaining two loops. This completes the stitch.

**6** Continue working into each stitch, until you reach the end of the row. Work the last stitch into the top of the turning chain of the previous row.

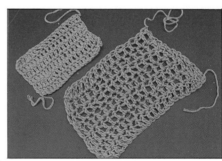

# FINISHING

**1** When the last stitch of the final row has been completed, cut the yarn and pull the end through the last loop on the hook. Pull it tight to secure the loop.

**2** Thread the loose end of yarn through a tapestry needle and sew it neatly into the back of the work.

Note: If you are left-handed, you may want to hold the hook in your left hand and the yarn in your right hand. If so, use these instructions reading "left" for "right" and "right" for "left" throughout. Hold the pictures up to a mirror and use the reflection.

# CROCHETING IN A ROUND

Crochet can be worked in a round, instead of rows, to make a tube.
Many simple items can be made from tubes: neckties, belts,
cushions, and bags.

## MAKING A TUBE

**1** Make a foundation chain. The number of stitches will vary according to what you are making. For the drawstring purse, cast on 55 chain stitches.

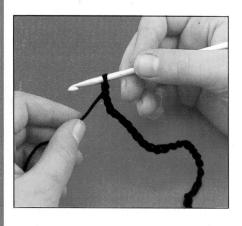

**2** Crochet one row in single crochet.

**3** Make the row into a ring by joining the first stitch to the last stitch with a **slip stitch**. To do this, pass the hook through the first stitch, bring the yarn over the hook, and draw a loop through both stitches. Be careful not to twist

the work as you make the slip stitch.

**4** Work a row of single crochet stitches around the tube. Keep crocheting around and around the tube until it is the right length. For the purse, it needs to be 8 inches from top to bottom.

**5** Work slip stitches into the next two stitches and finish off as usual.

## MAKING A DRAWSTRING PURSE

**1** Use the tube described here. Thread a tapestry needle with the same yarn and sew up the bottom of the tube using very small stitches.

**2** Thread the needle with yarn in a **contrasting** color. Sew large **running stitches** around the top to make a draw-string.

18

**3** Tie the ends of the drawstring together in a large knot.

# OTHER ITEMS

## 1 Headband
Make a foundation chain of 150 stitches. Crochet a short, fat tube about 1 inch wide.

## 2 Shoulder bag
Make a foundation chain of 200 stitches and crochet a large tube. Sew one end closed.

For the strap: Pass the hook through a stitch on the top edge of the bag. Using a new piece of yarn, draw a loop through the stitch, holding the loose end firmly. Double the yarn and make a chain stitch to draw the loose end through

the stitch. Make six single crochets along the edge.

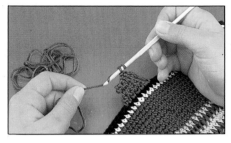

Work rows of single crochet to make a thin strap, about 32 inches long. Use slip stitches to attach it to the opposite edge of the bag. Work single crochet along the edges of the strap in a different color.

# MAKING COLORED STRIPES

**1** When starting a new row, draw the new yarn through to make a loop, instead of the old yarn.

**2** Secure the loose end of the new yarn by working over it when crocheting the next few stitches.

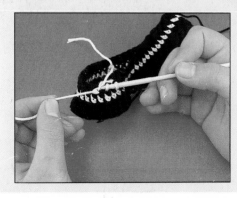

# MAKING COLORED PATTERNS

**1** When you wish to use a different color, pass the hook through the next stitch and use the new color to make the loop.

**2** Carry the old color along at the back of the work, until you want to use it again. Be careful not to pull the yarn too tight.

# A KNITTED PATCHWORK

In knitting, there are many different ways to combine purl and plain stitches to create different patterns and **textures**. Experiment by knitting small pieces in different stitches. Then sew the pieces together to make a patchwork wall hanging, bedcover, or cushion cover. Use what you learn about different stitches in future knitting projects.

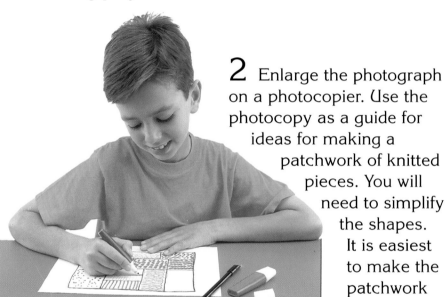

**1** Find a photograph like the one below, taken looking down from an airplane over a town or the countryside. This is called an aerial photograph. You will see that the fields in the photograph make up a pattern. They make a kind of patchwork of different colors, shapes, and textures.

**2** Enlarge the photograph on a photocopier. Use the photocopy as a guide for ideas for making a patchwork of knitted pieces. You will need to simplify the shapes. It is easiest to make the patchwork pieces all about the same size. Why not ask a group of friends to work with you, with each person knitting some of the pieces?

TURN TO PAGE 27 FOR IDEAS ABOUT WAYS OF COMBINING PURL AND PLAIN STITCHES.

**3** Select different yarns in a range of colors to match the colors in the photograph. Or work in black, white, and gray to match the photocopy.

**4** Knit a number of square and rectangular pieces. Cast on the number of stitches you need and experiment with plain and purl stitches to get the right texture.

**5** Crochet an edging around each piece. To do this, join in a new piece of yarn. Push the hook through the edge of the piece, from front to back, and draw a loop through, holding the loose end firmly. Make a chain stitch using the yarn double to

draw the loose end through the stitch (see shoulder bag on page 19).

**6** Work the edging in single crochet. To turn a corner, crochet two stitches into the same hole. Crochet a second row of edging in a different color.

**7** Sew the pieces together using a tapestry needle and matching yarn.

21

# A Crocheted Vest

This vest is pieced together from small, crocheted squares. This is a look that became fashionable in the early 1990s. In fact, this was a copy of a **hippie** fashion from the 1970s. And the hippies took the idea from the knitted or crocheted shawls and blankets made by the early European settlers in North America.

## To Make the Squares

1 Choose three yarns of the same thickness but different colors: A, B, C.

2 Using yarn A, make 6 chain stitches and join into a ring with a slip stitch.

3 **Round 1**
Make 3 chain stitches, then 2 double crochets into the ring. *Make 3 chain stitches then 3 double crochets into the ring. Repeat from * twice more. Then make 2 chain stitches and join with a slip stitch to the third of the first 3 chain stitches. Cut off the yarn, draw the end through the

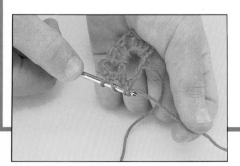

loop, and use the crochet hook to work the end into the back of the work.

4 **Round 2**
Join in yarn B by pushing the crochet hook through any of the four spaces.

Catch the yarn on the hook, holding the loose end firmly, and draw it through the space. Make a chain stitch using the yarn double (see shoulder bag on page 19) to draw the loose end through the stitch. Make 3 chain stitches, then 2 double crochets, 3 chain stitches then 3 double crochets, all into the same space.
*Make 1 chain stitch, then

3 double crochets, 3 chain stitches and 3 double crochets, all into the next space. Repeat from * twice more. Make 1 chain stitch and join with a slip stitch to the third of the first 3 chains. Break off the yarn and secure as in round 1.

5 **Round 3**
Join in yarn C to any 3-chain space. Make 3 chain stitches, followed by 2 double crochets, 3 chain stitches and then 3 double crochets, all into the same space. *Make 1 chain stitch, then make 3 double crochets into the next 1-chain space. Make 1 chain stitch, then make 3 double crochets, 3 chain stitches and 3 double crochets, all into the next 3-chain space.

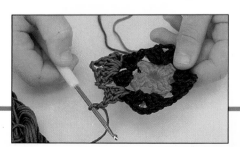

Repeat from * twice more. Make 1 chain stitch and join with a slip stitch to the third of the first 3 chains. Break off the yarn and secure.

# 6 Round 4

Join in yarn B to a 3-chain space. Make 3 chain stitches, then 2 double crochets, 3 chain stitches and 3 double crochets, all

into the same space. *(Make 1 chain stitch, followed by 3 double crochets into the next 1-chain space, then 1 chain stitch), repeat the instructions in parentheses in the next 1-chain space; make 3 double crochets, 3 chain stitches and 3 double crochets into the next 3-chain space. Repeat from * twice more. Then make 1 chain stitch, followed by 3 double crochets into the next 1-chain space, twice. Make 1 chain stitch and join it with a slip stitch to the third of the first 3 chains. Break off the yarn; secure.

# TO MAKE UP THE VEST

1 Make 32 squares as described. You might want to iron them. **Ask an adult to help you with the iron.**

2 Use yarn B to thread a tapestry needle. Sew together 16 squares to make a large square for the

back of the vest. Use 8 squares each to make two rectangles for the front of the vest.

3 With right sides together, sew the front sections to the back at the shoulders. Only sew halfway along, to leave space for your neck.

4 Sew up the sides. Start halfway up the first square and continue to the end of the second square. This gives room for movement and for your arms.

5 Finish off the armholes and edges of the vest by picking up the stitches with the crochet hook and making rows of single crochet stitches in different colors.

Note: The vest in these pictures was made using 3 1/2 ounces of yarn B and 1 ounce each of four different colors for yarns A and C. An E crochet hook was used. To make a bigger vest, use a thicker yarn or a larger crochet hook.

# KNITTING A SCARF

Throughout the centuries, knitting has been used to make items for keeping people warm. The yarn used for knitting is itself a good **insulator**, because the tiny fibers in it trap air. Air is also trapped between the knitted stitches. This trapped air keeps the body from losing heat.

Warm mittens, gloves, socks, and hats have been knitted in Europe ever since the craft was first introduced. In Great Britain, knitted caps were popular from medieval times on. In the sixteenth century, for example, the Welsh town of Monmouth was famous for producing knitted caps that soldiers wore under their helmets.

Making a scarf is a good way to practice your knitting. The most important thing is to keep the **tension** even from beginning to end. The tension depends on how tightly or loosely you pull the yarn as you knit. If the tension is not even, the edges of the scarf will go in and out, instead of being straight.

1 Cast on 50 stitches.

2 Decide on one pattern of stitches and stick to it throughout. Ribbing is often used for scarves because it looks the same on both sides. This scarf has been knitted using two purl and two plain stitches alternately.

3 Use different colors to make wide or narrow stripes. Remember, though, that all the yarn you use must be of a similar thickness. You could also use a yarn that has different colors in it, as shown here. Skeins of the same color should have matching dye lot numbers.

**7** Fold the pieces in half and thread the folded ends through the end of the scarf. It may help to use a crochet hook. Draw the loose ends through the loop to secure each tassel. Make a row of tassels in this way.

**4** When you have knitted the scarf to the length you want, cast off neatly.

**5** Add **tassels** to both ends. Wind yarn around a small box seven times.

**6** Cut through the yarn at one end. This will give you seven pieces of equal length.

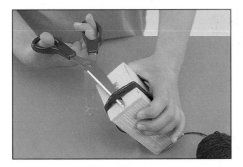

# DESIGN IDEAS

Reading a knitting pattern can be difficult at first, but it gets easier with practice. Knitting patterns use a special system of short instructions to guide the knitter row by row. This means that even very complicated instructions can be written down in a small space.

| | |
|---|---|
| k | knit |
| p | purl |
| st | stitch |
| dec | decrease |
| inc | increase |
| * | repeat the following instruction from this point |
| ( ) | repeat all the instructions in the parentheses as many times as instructed |
| sl | slip stitch (insert the right needle in the stitch in the usual way, slip it off the left needle onto the right needle without winding around the yarn) |
| psso | pass slipped stitch over the next stitch and off the needle |
| rep | repeat |
| tog | together |
| tbl | through back of loop |
| purlwise | put the needle through the stitch as if to purl |
| knitwise | put the needle through the stitch as if to knit a plain stitch |

Once you know how to read a pattern you can make all kinds of things. You can buy knitting patterns from fabric and yarn stores and craft stores. Or you may find them in craft magazines. Here is a list of knitting instructions with their explanations, plus instructions for some other stitches you might like to try.

▲ *A row counter is useful when following a complicated pattern. Turn the counter one notch after finishing each row.*

26

## 1 Moss stitch (above)

Cast on a multiple of 2 stitches. Row 1: *k1, p1, rep from * to end.
Row 2: *p1, k1, rep from * to end.
Repeat rows 1 and 2.

## 2 Broken garter stitch

Cast on a multiple of 6 stitches, plus 5 stitches.
Row 1: k to end.
Row 2: k5, *p1, k5, rep from * to end.
Repeat rows 1 and 2.

## 3 Simple basket pattern

Cast on a multiple of 4 stitches, plus 2 stitches.
Row 1: k2, *p2, k2, rep from * to end.
Row 2: *k2, p2, rep from * to end. Repeat rows 1 and 2.

## 4 Three-by-three rib

Cast on a multiple of 6 stitches, plus 3 stitches.
Row 1: *k3, p3, rep from * to last 3 stitches, k3.
Row 2: p3, *k3, p3, rep from * to end.
Repeat rows 1 and 2.

## 5 Knife-pleat rib

Cast on a multiple of 13 stitches.
Row 1: *k4, (p1,k1) 3 times, p3, rep from * to end.
Row 2: *k3, (p1,k1) 3 times, p4, rep from * to end.
Repeat rows 1 and 2.

## 6 Twisted fabric

Cast on an even number of stitches.
Row 1: k to end.
Row 2: p to end.
Row 3: k1, *sl1, k1, psso, but k in back of the slip st before slipping it off the left needle, rep from * to last st, k1.
Row 4: p to end.
Row 5: k2, rep from * of row 3 to last 2 sts, k2.
Repeat rows 2 to 5.

## 7 Twisted ringwood

Cast on a multiple of 2 stitches, plus 1 stitch.
Row 1: k into the back of all stitches to end.
Row 2: k1, *p1, k1, rep from * to end.
Repeat rows 1 and 2.

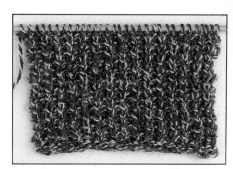

# THE GALLERY

There are two main ways of adding interest to your knitting and crochet: first, you can use different colors to make a pattern or picture; second, you can use different stitches to produce different textures.

Collect ideas about color and texture for your work by looking carefully at the world around you. Notice how light effects the color and pattern of an object. The same things can look quite different depending on the time of the day or the season of the year. When light strikes a surface from the side, it shows up all the bumps and ridges. When a light is shone from above, the surface may seem flat, but the color looks deeper and richer.

Cut out interesting pictures from magazines, collect cards and postcards, and take your own photographs. These pictures will give you some ideas.

▲ A fancy mosaic

◄ Carved stonework

A tiled wall ▶

▲ *A stone wall*

◀ *A domed roof*

▲ *Fields of flowers*

◀ *Patterns in sand*

▼ *A patchwork of fields*

# GLOSSARY

**Apprenticeship** A period of learning a skill or trade, usually by working for someone who is already qualified and who passes on their knowledge.

**Contrasting** Things "contrast" when they are very unlike one another.

**Decreasing** Making smaller. In knitting, decreasing usually means knitting stitches together to leave fewer stitches on the needle.

**Fashion designers** People who think up new styles in clothing.

**Felting** A method of making cloth from woolen fibers. Wool has tiny hooks on each fiber. When the fibers are dampened and rubbed the hooks mesh together to form felt cloth.

**Fibers** The tiny threads used to make cloth.

**Guilds** Kinds of clubs or associations. In medieval Europe, people who worked in a particular craft joined together to form a guild. The guilds looked after the well-being of all members and tried to make sure standards of work remained high.

**Hippie** One of a loose grouping of people who share the same ideas about their way of life, food, clothes and so on, and who disagree with many traditional customs and behavior. The first hippies lived in the United States and Europe in the 1960s.

**Increasing** Making bigger. In knitting, increasing usually means knitting twice into the same stitch, to make more stitches on the needle.

**Insulator** Something that stops the transfer of heat.

**Ivory** The hard, white substance that elephant's tusks are made of. In the past, many elephants were killed for their ivory, which was used to make jewelry and other items. Today, to protect the world's elephants, it is against the law to buy or sell new ivory.

**Medieval** Relating to the Middle Ages.

**Middle Ages** A period of history in Europe lasting from about the fifth to the fifteenth century.

**Needles** In knitting, these are slender rods around which the yarn is wound to make the stitches.

**Patterns** In knitting, crochet, or sewing, patterns are plans or sets of instructions for making something.

**Professional** Done as a way of earning a living.

**Right sides** In knitting and sewing, the sides of the work that will be seen when it is finished. The other sides, which will not be seen, are called the wrong sides.

**Running stitches** Simple sewing stitches in which the needle is passed in and out of the cloth to make a line of even-sized stitches.

**Seams** The lines along which pieces of cloth are sewn together.

**Sheath** A case or covering.

**Slipknot** A loose knot that will slide along the thread on which it is tied.

**Slip stitch** In crochet, a stitch that joins two other stitches together.

**Tassels** Tufts of loose threads used to decorate the edge of a piece of cloth.

**Tension** The extent to which something, such as a thread or piece of yarn, is stretched.

**Textiles** All kinds of cloth.

**Textures** The feel of surfaces of materials or objects.
**Tradition** A custom that has been practiced over many years, by one generation of people after another.

**Unravel** To undo or unwind.
**Weaving** A way of making cloth by crisscrossing horizontal and vertical threads.

# FURTHER INFORMATION

## CROCHET ABBREVIATIONS

The following are abbreviations you will run into when following instructions to crochet:

| | | | | | |
|---|---|---|---|---|---|
| ch | chain | ch- | previously made chain stitch | | |
| dc | double crochet | dec | decrease | inc | increase |
| lp | loop | rep | repeat | sc | single crochet |
| sl st | slip stitch | sp | space | st | stitch |
| tch | turning chain | tog | together | yo | yarn over |

## BOOKS TO READ

Baker, Wendy. *Knitting.* Hands-On (New York: Thomson Learning, 1994).

Lawler, T. *Sewing and Knitting* (Tulsa, OK: EDC Publishing, 1979).

Messent, Jan. *Wool 'n Magic: Creative Uses of Yarn* (Woodstock, NY: Arthur Schwartz & Co., 1989).

O'Reilly, Susie. *Textiles.* Technology Projects (New York: Bookwright Press, 1991).

For the left-handed, two simple booklets – *The Left-Hander's Guide to Knitting* and *The Left-Hander's Guide to Crochet* (published by Left-Handers International) – are available from: Left-Handers International, P.O. Box 8249, Topeka, KS 66608 (tel: 913/234-2177).

**For further information, contact:**

The American Craft Council
72 Spring Street
New York, NY 10012

The Knitting Guild of America
P.O. Box 1606
Knoxville, TN 37901

Crochet Association International
P.O. Box 131
Dallas, GA 30132

# INDEX

# ACKNOWLEDGMENTS

The publishers would like to thank the following for allowing their photographs to be reproduced: Crafts Council *title page*, 4 left; Eye Ubiquitous 4 right, 9 top left (P. Seheult), 9 bottom (Y. Nikiteas), 9 top right (R. Nottridge), 29 top left (P. Thompson); Hamburger Kunsthalle, Germany 6 left (E. Walford); Horizon 5 bottom (D. Simmonds); Hulton Deutsch Collection Limited 7 right; Images Color Library 28 top right, 28 bottom right, 29 center left, 29 top right, 29 bottom right; Leicestershire Museums, Art Galleries, and Records Service 6 right; 7 top left, 8 right; Life File 7 bottom left (G. Burns), 28 bottom left (E. Wilkins); ZEFA 5 top (Halina), 20 left, 29 bottom left (Allstock). All other photographs were supplied by Zul Mukhida. Logo artwork was supplied by John Yates. The author would like to thank Ailsa O'Reilly and Ethel Tapp for their advice and help.

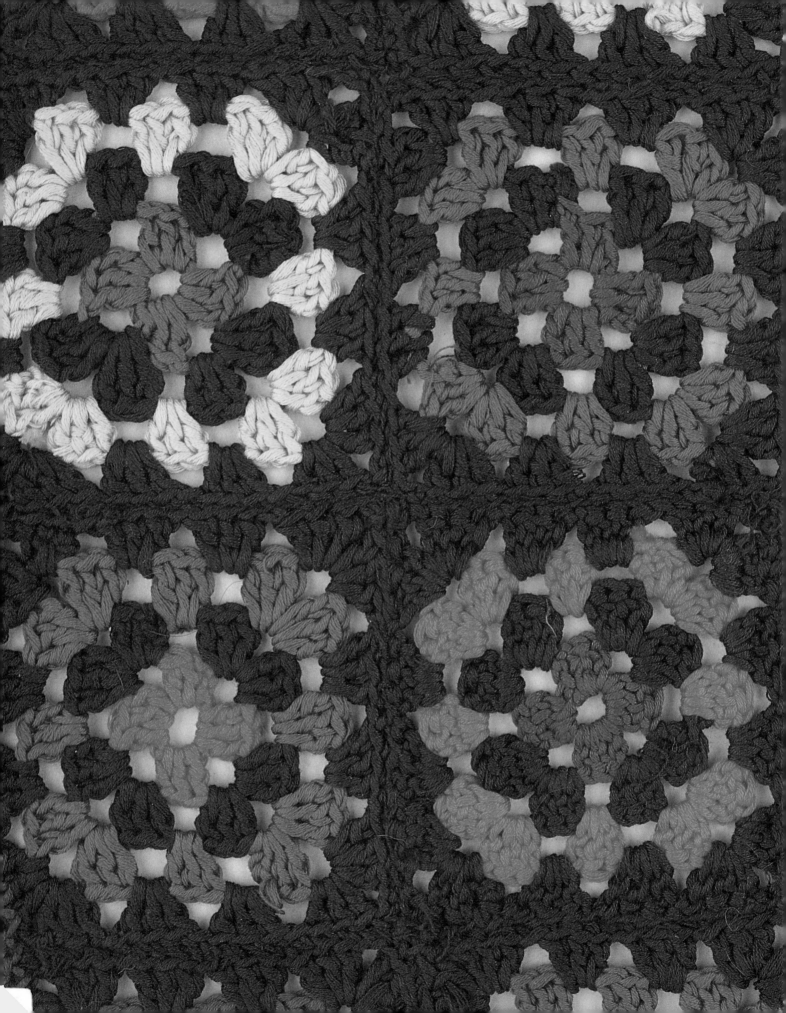